Maximus
has a bad day

First published 1996.

Scripture Union, 207–209 Queensway,
Bletchley, Milton Keynes MK2 2EB, England.

ISBN 1 85999 057 6

Designed by Tony Cantale Graphics.

Printed in Singapore by Tien Wah Press.

Maximus
has a bad day

Brian Ogden

Illustrated by Elke Counsell

Scripture Union

‘You’ve given me the wrong change,’ said Maximus to the girl mouse on the checkout. ‘I gave you a ten pound note and you’ve only given me change for a fiver.’

‘Excuse me, sir,’ she said, ‘but here is the note you gave me. Look it’s only five pounds.’

Maximus had been shopping and it had taken him ages to make up his mind what he wanted to buy. Should he take Whizz Pops with a plastic dinosaur in the packet or Wheaty Wonders with a water pistol? He got in another muddle over some cheese he especially wanted for a party. By the time he got to the checkout he was in a really bad mood.

‘Oh, all right,’ said Maximus crossly. ‘I suppose I’ve got to believe you, but I’m sure it was a ten pound note.’

BRING FUN
INTO SHOPPING!
WHIZZ
POPS

Maximus went down the road towards the bus station and, just as he was walking over the badger crossing, the handle broke on his plastic carrier bag. His coffee jar rolled off under a parked car and his other shopping lay in an unhappy pile.

Suddenly, there was a loud hoot and Maximus leapt in the air. It was the driver of a bus who had hooted. All the passengers were laughing at him trying to collect his belongings. That wasn't the only problem.

The bus that had stopped was the bus he wanted and he had to wait another half-hour for the next one.

39
39
JFEC - 95

Just as he turned into the churchyard gate he saw Patrick, his friend who also lived at St Michael's, coming out of the door.

'Had a good afternoon, Maximus?' asked Patrick politely.

'No,' said Maximus.

'Sorry to hear that. What's the problem?'

'Mind your own business,' answered Maximus rudely and stamped off into the church. He took his shopping into the vestry and put it all away. As he did so, he looked again at the coffee jar – 'Bistro Gravy Browning' it said on the label. 'Oh no!' shouted Maximus. 'I can't even have a cup of coffee now.'

He flung himself on his paper handkerchief duvet and lay there in a really boiling temper. Suddenly, there was a loud bang on the vestry window. Maximus leapt off his duvet and scampered through his special hole in the wall. Just outside the window he saw a whole crowd of Patrick's children. They were playing football. It was the ball which had hit the window. Maximus marched into the middle of the group of children and picked it up.

15
46
4
2

‘That’s the last time you disturb me with this!’ he shouted at them, and stormed back to the vestry carrying the ball. It was a struggle to get through the hole with the football in his paws and he knocked one knee on the bricks which did nothing to make him feel any happier.

Maximus went through the vestry into the church. As he walked down the aisle he heard a whooshing noise and felt the wind blowing in his fur. He knew at once that it was Barnabas.

'Barnabas, you beastly bat, stop it!' said Maximus angrily. 'This is no place for low flying.'

'But Maximus, I'm practising for the Bats of Britain Air Show. You know, next week when the Red Sparrows are coming.'

'Well, not here and not now! This is a church and not an airport. Leave me in peace and practise somewhere else.'

St. Michael's
Choir

Just as the bat flew out of the church, Johann Sebastian – the organist's cat – came in to fetch some music. Johann was a friendly animal and he and Maximus usually got on well. Johann was very musical and even liked Bach, after whom the organist has named him.

'What do you want?' asked Maximus crossly. 'I've just got rid of a bat and now here's a cat – I suppose it'll be a rat next!'

'I'm sorry if I disturbed you – just fetching a hymn book,' replied Johann politely. 'I shan't be long, then you can have the church to yourself again.' Maximus stamped off and soon the cat left.

'Nobody to talk to,' said Maximus to himself. 'Thought church animals were supposed to be friendly but here I am on my own again. Nobody understands that a mouse can get lonely – they all go off and leave me. Anybody would think they didn't want to see me.'

He went into the pulpit to see if there were any sermon notes to have for tea. Sermon notes were his favourite – somehow they tasted specially good. Sure enough, lying in the pulpit were several delicious-looking sheets. Maximus glanced at the top of the first one and began to read what it said. 'John chap. 15 verse 12, "Love one another, just as I love you."'

'I don't know who this John chap is but it certainly makes you think,' said Maximus to himself. 'Love each other ... er, I'm not very good at that.'

Johann Sebastian
Barnabas
checkout girl
Patrick

‘I didn’t believe the girl mouse on the checkout at the shop, I was rude to Patrick, unkind to the children with the ball, and very nasty to both Barnabas and Johann. It isn’t really surprising they don’t want to see me. This John chap says love one another – I really must try a lot harder.’ And Maximus went off to say sorry to them all.

Heavenly Father,
We have days when everything goes wrong
and then we are unkind and hurt other people.
Forgive us when this happens and help us
to love them as you love us.
Amen.